AQUARIUMS

BY JOHN HOKE

Aquariums

FRANKLIN WATTS | NEW YORK | LONDON

◄—A FIRST BOOK—►

Cover by Seymour Schlatner

The author gratefully acknowledges the photo
assistance of the Fish Nest, Bethesda, Maryland.

Library of Congress Cataloging in Publication Data

Hoke, John, 1925-
    Aquariums.

    (A First book)
    SUMMARY: Describes different kinds of
aquariums, how to set them up, and how to care
for them.
    Bibliography: p.
    1. Aquariums–Juvenile literature. [1. Aquar-
iums] I. Title.
SF457.H598 1975   639'.34   74-9834
ISBN 0-531-02772-4

7 6 5 4 3

CONTENTS

AQUARIUMS

WHAT IS AN AQUARIUM?

A rectangle of glass or plastic becomes an aquarium when it is filled with water, planted with appropriate plants, and has animal life added to it in such a way that the life flourishes as it would in its own natural environment. The successful aquarium is an operating ecosystem wherein all the needs of the life are met sufficiently to allow it to live in such an encapsulated world.

BASIC TYPES
OF AQUARIUMS

Whatever the size or shape of the container, the use of aquariums as home environments for living plants and creatures of the water will fall into one of the following categories.

THE COMMUNITY TANK is one of the more popular kinds of aquariums for it allows many kinds of tropical fish to be seen living together harmoniously in a single tank.

THE ONE-SPECIES AQUARIUM is one that displays a group limited to one species of fish, particularly those that stick closely together — or *school* — as they move about in a constant flow of color.

THE BREEDERS AQUARIUM is the dream of every aquarist who has

so well cared for the fish he keeps that they reproduce. This aquarium provides the fish with a tank of their own for the breeding period.

THE NURSERY TANK serves as a special haven for raising the young that are produced by breeders. Fish are not always good parents away from their natural environment.

THE SALT WATER AQUARIUM contains sea water — and the beautiful creatures of the ocean.

BASIC REQUIREMENTS
FOR A
HEALTHY AQUARIUM

Setting up an aquarium requires knowledge of the needs of the living things that will inhabit it. To be the most attractive while being the easiest to maintain, an aquarium should be able to function as an almost complete ecosystem. This ideal calls for a physical environment in which all the living things put into the aquarium can find both a home — what scientists call a *niche* — and all the physical factors that are vital to their existence. In the natural environment a life form cannot live if any *one* vital physical factor is missing. This rule is no less true in an aquarium — which becomes a home away from home for the fish and other life put into it.

PHYSICAL FACTORS IN THE AQUARIUM ENVIRONMENT

The physical factors that are important to living things in an aquarium are light, temperature, chemical make-up of the water, aeration and movement of the water, water cleanliness, space for living things, and bottom soil conditions.

LIGHT plays a vital role in an aquarium, quite aside from making it look attractive. When there is bright light the plants growing in an aquarium provide oxygen in the water, they recycle the wastes that fall and are buried in the bottom gravel, and they provide shelter for the fish. In the absence of light the plants consume oxygen. Fish and other life in the aquarium need oxygen just as do other creatures. They extract oxygen from the water through their gills. Aeration of water is also accomplished in other ways, but the presence of plants that generate oxygen, as a by-product of their food making in the presence of bright light, is part of the natural process. Aeration becomes particularly essential in a tank that has many fish in it. It is important to avoid keeping more fish in an aquarium than it can handle.

The role of light in the aquarium is just as vital as it is in the natural environment. And it is just about the most important chemical process in the world because it is the process that creates food for the primary consumers in all food chains upon which all life depends.

In the aquarium, the light enables the water plantlife to convert carbon dioxide (CO_2), many inorganic chemicals, and water into the organic materials that make up the plants themselves. This process is known as photosynthesis. In the aquarium, this process helps reduce many of the wastes the other life forms release into the system as a process of their own living. In bright light the plants contribute some oxygen to the system while removing the waste CO_2 the animal life releases into the water (most of which is of course exchanged, as a physical process, at the water's surface through aeration).

WATER TEMPERATURE is an important factor for the life in a water environment. Many fish are restricted to a fairly narrow temperature range. Most aquarium store fish come from warm-water environments. They are fish whose home temperatures range from 70° to 85°F, and they are usually sensitive to rapid changes in their water temperature.

CHEMICAL MAKEUP of aquarium water is also an important consideration. The overall acid-alkaline range acceptable to almost all fish is reasonably broad, but if they are to be seen at their best, their water must be adjusted to the acid-alkalinity range most suited to them. The chemistry symbol pH is one that deals with the amount of hydrogen ions in water, which in turn (depending on the amount) indicates the acid-alkaline nature of the water. As with all methods of measuring, scientists use numbers to measure the amounts between the extremes of what they are measuring. In the case of measuring pH, the point at which water is neutral — neither acid nor basic — is number 7 on the pH scale. By and large, the pH range within which most tropical fish live is about 6.4 and 7.8.

Simple tools for determining the pH of water are sold in aquarium stores, along with the chemicals and information needed to correct aquarium water not at the right pH level.

AERATION AND WATER MOVEMENT is necessary if animal life is to survive in water. Plantlife provides a limited amount of aeration. But most aquarium enthusiasts wish to keep more fish in their tanks than the vegetation can support with oxygen. In such cases other means are needed to provide adequate air for them.

By keeping the aquarium water in constant circulation, waste gases (mainly CO_2) are able to leave the water at the surface and oxygen is brought into the water. Pumping or bubbling air through the water lifts it to the surface where the gas exchange takes place.

Water movement is also important as a means of giving active fish in a small aquarium a means of exercising. They can swim into the current of water. But, equally important, there should be places of quiet in the tank — behind shelves of rock, or in vegetation where even active fish can rest where the water is still.

CLEANLINESS is important in an aquarium. A basic cycle takes place where illumination causes plants to manufacture food and to grow. As part of the process, wastes absorbed into the gravel in an aquarium are recycled. The work performed by light is helped by many microorganisms that live in the water and soil (or gravel) in the bottom of the aquarium. Many of the wastes released by the fish, and other life, cannot be used directly by the plants as part of the photosynthesis process. Certain forms of bacteria and other minute life consume these wastes as part of *their* living process. They convert the wastes into the minerals and other inorganic materials the plantlife draws from its environment in order to grow. It is a recycling process, for some of these same materials began their movement through the food chain: From earth (and the water surrounding the water plants) — to plants (some of the plant material, itself, drops off) — to animals that feed on the plants, droppings from the animals — to other animals that prey on each other, and small dead animals themselves. All these materials are at some point "processed" by the microorganisms and the inorganic "building blocks" returned to the form in which the plants can utilize them as part of their growing process.

In earth, this process takes place in the soil, and works in a like manner in the watery environment. In the aquarium these organisms are present in the water as well. For cleanliness, and where more fish and other animal life are present, gravel is used in place of soil.

A special water filter is often used in an aquarium to keep the water clear and to help aerate it.

SPACE in an aquarium is important. In the natural environment, each life form's niche involves an adequate measure of space. Many fish are quite determined about finding their place in an aquarium, which then becomes their territory and which they will jealously guard. Needless to say if the aquarium cannot provide adequate space for each fish's territorial needs, there will be disturbances. Space and oxygen requirements are an important factor in deciding on what fish to buy and what size aquarium to set up.

BOTTOM COVER — soil, gravel, or perhaps none at all — is the last important physical consideration. In the natural environment, "bottom" is often silt that is rich in nutrients that can support both submerged plants and those that break water, grow, and blossom above the surface. Silt in an aquarium is a problem, for any movement of the water will stir it up and cloud the aquarium. So a choice of loose gravel instead of rich silt is best for maintaining a clear-water aquarium. Plantlife will not suffer for nutrients. The droppings from fish and other animal life in the aquarium enriches the water around the gravel, and the roots in the gravel are able to draw upon this source of nourishment as the water flows through the gravel.

LIFE FORMS
IN AN
AQUARIUM

As we have seen, plants perform several important functions in an aquarium. The more plants there are, the more effectively these natural processes will be performed. Not all the bottom area of the aquarium should be planted, however, for you will want some room for the fish.

Most of the plants sold in aquarium stores are of the kind that live out their lives beneath the surface of the water. Most aquarium lights rest on the rims of the aquarium or completely cover the top of the tank, so there's little room for plants that grow above the water. Unless you've a special purpose, subsurface plants sold in aquarium stores are the best to use.

LIVING "HOUSECLEANERS" in an aquarium are quite important. Snails and certain bottom-feeding fish help keep the aquarium clean by eating scraps of uneaten food. They make maintaining an aquarium much easier. Some forms of this life will also feed upon algae (simple green plants) that may grow on the glass sides of the tank, cutting down on the time you must devote to wiping it off the glass, in order to see inside.

The last life form to be placed in the aquarium is the fish. Once the aquarium is functioning well — and all physical considerations are well in hand — the fish chosen to live in the system can be purchased and carefully introduced into the system.

SETTING UP
AN AQUARIUM

A trip to an aquarium store will help you decide the kinds of fish you will want to keep, and hence what size aquarium to buy. As far as tank maintenance is concerned, a larger system is about as easy to care for as a small one. It is also less likely to go foul as quickly as will a small one. And the choice of fish that will live in a large tank is more varied than it is for a small tank. Once you've picked the tank you want, buy the amount of gravel and the other materials the dealer suggests you'll need to set up the aquarium. Whatever size aquarium you buy, buy *all* the components needed at the same time. Don't economize by doing without a heater or filter. They are important to the system; so much so that aquarium dealers often sell complete systems at a reduced rate.

THE TANK is the first important component of the aquarium. A tank must be moved very carefully. When put in a car, be sure it rests on a *flat* surface — preferably a sheet of plywood, if the car trunk or station wagon deck isn't smooth.

New or used, you are going to want to clean the aquarium, and this is a good time to make sure it doesn't leak. Put it on a flat surface in the basement, laundry room, or elsewhere where leaking water won't hurt anything, and where you can easily siphon off or ladle out the water you put into it. Fill the tank to the rim, to both rinse it out and check it for leaks. (Don't use any soap in the wash water!) Should you spy a leak in a used tank try to find the point where it is coming out of a seam. You can seal the leak up while water is in the tank by caulking over the leaking seam with silastic rubber (sold in tubes by most aquarium or hardware stores). The water pressure will force the sealant deep into the leak area.

The rinsed tank, free of leaks, should be located on a flat surface that you *know* can support the weight of the tank when it is full of water. The water in a twenty-gallon tank will weigh over 160 pounds! By the time the tank's weight is added in, along with a light housing, filter, etc., a twenty-gallon system will be pushing 200 pounds — or the equivalent of the weight of a full-grown man. A bookcase or table must be sturdy and substantial to bear up under such a weight. If you can afford a metal tank stand, specially constructed to hold the aquarium, it will provide an attractive support and perhaps have shelving beneath it for all the necessary gear, fish food, books, etc., you will accumulate.

BOTTOM COVER is the next consideration. When a sturdy, flat location for the tank has been found, the tank should be partially filled with water. Before the aquarium gravel is put in the tank, thoroughly rinse the gravel with running water. The best way to do this is to place the gravel in a bucket and use the garden hose. (Outdoors, in the yard is the place for this operation.) Run water through the gravel to the pail bottom — until the water overflowing the pail rim runs clean. Stir the gravel up constantly while washing it to hasten the process. Again: Use no soap or other cleaners. Just water!

The drained gravel is then ready to be ladled into the half-filled aquarium. If you plan to use a subsand filter, you must get it and its air hose in place on the bottom of the tank *before* adding the gravel.

In spite of the pains taken in cleaning the gravel, the water in the tank will still be a little cloudy at this point. You will continue clouding the water anyway as you are now ready to set plants into place. But the tank will soon clear when the filter is turned on.

SETTING IN THE PLANTS comes next. Many plants have a surprisingly small root structure so make sure that enough gravel is in place around their roots to secure them. Long and thin plants, like Vallisneria, make an ideal backdrop planted along the back of the aquarium. Low-growing broadleaf plants such as young Sword plants, and some members of the Cryptocoryne family should be singly planted and spaced so they can spread out as they grow. Certain plants make ideal centerpieces in a tank. The Amazon Sword Plant is one of these. Its broad leaves flare out to fill its central planting place.

Do all planting and gravel shifting while the aquarium is only partially full of water. This will keep spillage down. If you're using a subsurface filter — under the gravel — make sure gravel doesn't get dropped into its opening stem, which should protrude up through the gravel. An air hose operates this filter. It should be connected before putting in the gravel and plants. This will prevent the lower opening to the filter from being filled with gravel.

If an outside filter is to be used, it can be set up after the tank is full. If an inside box filter that rests on top of the gravel is to be used, locate it behind a screen of plants.

FILLING THE TANK follows planting. Add more water to just above the viewing level and start the filter system. Filters that hang on the outside of the tank are fed water from the tank by hook-shaped plastic siphon tubes. An air line, or water-turbine pump re-

VALLISNERIA

SWORD PLANT

turns water from the filter box back into the aquarium through another plastic tube. If this kind of filter is used, install it now.

HEATERS are needed to keep the aquarium at a fairly constant temperature. (75°F is usually the most desired level.) The aquarium store sells tubular, glass-enclosed, thermostatically controlled heaters to meet the needs of any size aquarium. Once installed in the tank and attached to the rim of the aquarium — and adjusted to the desired heat level — the heater will automatically maintain the aquarium water temperature at the selected setting.

WHAT KIND OF FILTER do you need?

Three kinds of filters are available for aquarium use. The subsoil filter discussed earlier is either a perforated sheet of plastic or a lattice of perforated tubing that is located on the tank bottom, *under* the gravel. An air line operates this filter, drawing water down through the gravel bottom, filtering out the dirt before the water is pumped back up into the tank.

The inside filter box is a plastic container that holds activated carbon and a cottonlike polyester filter "floss" that serves to screen particles out of water that is pumped through it — and the charcoal — by an air line. It can be located anywhere in the aquarium below the surface of the water, hidden behind a piece of rock or a thicket of plants.

Outside filter boxes hang on the outside rim of the aquarium. They are the best to use for large aquariums. Many kinds use a motor-driven turbine pump that flows considerable water through the filter. Its greater output, ease of cleaning, and outside location that makes changing easy, are all advantages. Siphon tubes flow water out of the tank into the filter, and the pump drives it back into the tank after it has been cleansed by the filter material (the same as that used in the inside filter box).

ILLUMINATION FOR THE AQUARIUM is an important factor. Both tungsten and fluorescent lamps are used in aquarium lamp housings to enhance the appearance of plants and fish in the tank.

Setting up an aquarium:
Once the tank is clean
and leak-free, clean, washed
gravel can be put in the
tank. An inch or so deep is
plenty. If you want to make
a rock sculpture, put it in
place now — carefully, so
you do not scratch or break
the glass. If you plan to use
a subgravel filter, it goes in
first, and is then covered with
gravel. Take care not to drop
any gravel into the tubes
that extend above the gravel.

Fill the tank only half full of water before adding plants. This procedure will prevent sloshing water over the side while you carefully root-in each plant to create the green backdrop for your fish. When planting is done, top up the tank with water — taking care not to uproot the plants while pouring. Your hand, or a jar set in on the bottom can be used to break the pour stream.

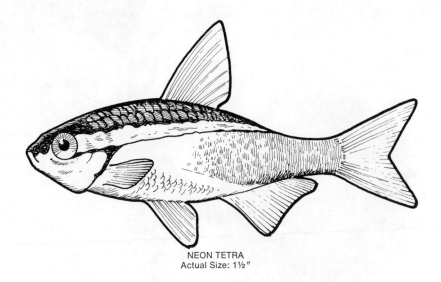

NEON TETRA
Actual Size: 1½″

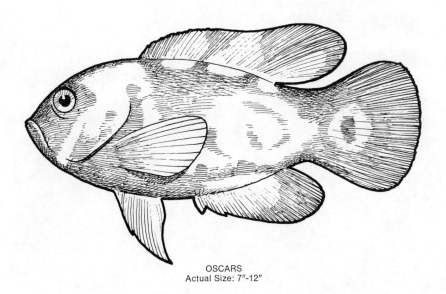

OSCARS
Actual Size: 7″-12″

With the lamp housing in place, heater on, and filter running, the process of tank preparation is complete. Hold off buying fish until the newly created aquarium has had time to settle down. Does it hold water (no leaks)? Does the filter function well? Is the heater holding the water temperature constant? Time must be allowed for any chlorine in the water to be aerated off. Many municipal water works inject chlorine into the city drinking water to destroy disease causing germs. But the chlorine can also destroy tropical fish! It is best to let the completed aquarium operate for at least two days before adding fish. Then, when everything is going well, is the time to put tropical fish into the aquarium.

WHAT KINDS OF FISH, AND HOW MANY are the next considerations. The urge to buy lots and lots of fish for your aquarium must be subdued: Too few is better than too many. There is no hard and fast rule as to how many fish you can keep in a tank. It can range from a need of several square inches of water surface for each *small* guppy, to at least fifty gallons of water for a pair of adult Oscars (*Astronotus ocellatus*). Until you gain experience, follow the advice of the aquarium shop proprietor, or you will run the risk of killing everything on your first try!

While waiting several days for your new aquarium to settle down, you may wish to visit the aquarium store and look over and price the fish. In general, the more ornate and larger, majestic fish cost more, but you will also note that small ones such as the brilliant Cardinal tetra are fairly expensive. Novelty and extravagant coloration always tends to enhance the price of any fish. Pay particular attention to what *you* find attractive, rather than to which cost more. When you've settled upon the varieties that please you most, learn which of these are the easiest to care for, and which kinds will get along together!

DO YOUR HOMEWORK and your aquarium will benefit. Now is the time to look over the aquarium store's display of pamphlets and books about tropical fish (and those in your school library). Many

Aquarium equipment: If you use a turbine filter, it can be hung on the back of the aquarium. After starting the siphon tubes that flow the water out of the tank into the filter box, it will fill with water. Turn it on now so that it can start cleaning the tank. If you plan to use an air-driven inside box filter, it should be located in a corner on the bottom. The air pump will pull water through its filtering material. Some tanks use a glass cover and lamp assembly to close the top of the tank. Once the tank has been set up, put the cover in place.

There are a great many products available to help the aquarist succeed and enjoy the aquarium hobby. The shop proprietor will help you select those things that are going to be the most useful: Remember that your main objective is to keep tropical fish in your aquarium, so every cent you spend on a piece of equipment you may not really need will reduce your funds for fish purchases.

describe in detail the living behavior and needs of a great variety of tropical fish. You may hesitate to spend the money you planned for fish purchases on reading matter, but it is a good investment to buy at least one publication that will help you through your early days of aquarium keeping. There are a number of very fine, well illustrated books and pamphlets available. Remember: Each fish that perishes in your tank, because you didn't know enough about its needs, is money lost — quite aside from having been a distinct unkindness to the unfortunate fish, if its demise is your fault!

HAVE A CHAT WITH THE AQUARIUM STORE PROPRIETOR to get some helpful advice. With a little reading behind you, talk with the aquarium store proprietor. If he helped you select the aquarium you have set up, he can also help you select the fish to go in it. Trust his judgment. Most dealers will try to make sure your first experiences with an aquarium are successful, so listen to their advice when you make your first purchase.

THE CRITICAL MOMENT

Putting your fish into the aquarium calls for careful technique. You mustn't just dump them in. You will have returned from the aquarium store with one or several plastic bags of fish in some water that came from their tank in the store. Devote your first attention to temperature. If you made your purchase in the wintertime, carry the bags of fish in a cardboard box or other well-insulated container to protect them from the winter weather. In the summer, sunlight must not heat the bags of water.

Before the fish go into the aquarium, the water they are to go into must be the same temperature as the water in which you brought them home. To match up the bag and aquarium temperatures float the bags in the aquarium until the water in the bag is the same temperature as the water in the tank. Prick a small hole in the bags when you do this — clipping them to the rim of the tank, and then check the bag temperature and the tank temperature from time to time. Make sure the bags are deep enough inside the tank so that the fish cannot jump out. When the temperatures match, loose the fish into the tank as gently as possible, allowing the fish to swim into their new home.

But first check the pH of their water. If neither the water they're in nor that of the tank is ideal for them, bring the tank level to that of the water in the bag. Use a pH kit to determine the reading, and then add the proper chemicals to the tank to make the pH change. After the fish have been in their new home for a while, you can then adjust the pH factor of their water to the correct level. The aquarium store proprietor can advise you about how to use the pH kit and the chemicals properly.

WATCH THE FISHES' BEHAVIOR after you put them into your tank. They may become quite pale or discolored, hiding in some corner in obvious fear. Should they start darting about — striking the glass or objects in the tank — turn out the tank lights and the room lights to make their new quarters as dim as possible. Until the newcomers settle down, don't release any remaining bagged fish. In time, the more skittish fish will calm down, as they become accustomed to their new home. Until all the fish are quite at home, leave the tank light off. The "instant daylight" their tank light creates is startling to them during their adjustment to their new home. Once they feel at home they will adjust to abrupt lighting situations.

FEEDING is an important matter. It is tempting to think that the fishes' first need is food, but it isn't true. Rest, while they adjust, is their first need. In a day or two, when they have settled down you can then try adding a little food. If they eat it, fine. If they don't, wait another day before adding more food.

HEALTH PROBLEMS can crop up after a transfer. Watch for any illness that might crop up because of the turmoil of being bagged, carted about, and introduced to strange waters. Fish are usually at their weakest then and certain diseases are quick to develop, such as a skin parasite sometimes called "Ick" after the parasite's long name, Ichthyophthirius. In this condition many tiny white spots appear all over the fish. A gradual rise of the water's temperature to 85°F is the first part of the remedy. Then obtain some Methylene Blue (in a 5 percent aqueous solution) to add to the tank water at a rate of two drops per gallon of water. (This treatment must take place in a separate container since the chemical can kill aquarium plants.) The aquarium store proprietor can supply it, and help you overcome such health hurdles.

With care you need not experience these problems. Keep the fishes' new home in top shape, and the possibility of illness caused by the move will diminish.

AQUARIUM LIFE-SUPPORT EQUIPMENT AND WHAT IT DOES

Once an aquarium has begun to function properly, the plants grow quickly and the tropical fish and other forms of animal life thrive. The lamp above the tank illuminates the scene in a way that makes it seem almost like a theater. Once accustomed to people peering in at them, the fish tend almost to ignore viewers. At this point the system is at its best. But while everything seems to take care of itself, a lot of natural forces are at work — such as plant growth, aeration, and the recycling of waste materials. It is the special equipment in and on your tank which enables it to support the life in it away from its natural environment. Each piece of equipment plays an important role in controlling the vital physical factors that create a successful aquarium.

THE HEATER AND THERMOMETER are essential equipment.

In the lakes and streams of tropical lands, water bodies are large, the sun and earth warmth is greater, and so the water temperature is also higher and relatively constant.

Life from these waters in an aquarium in your living room must enjoy the same unchanging warmth. But your living room temperature varies, and an aquarium heater is needed to keep the water temperature at the level the tropical life requires.

It works much like the heating system in your home. Any drop in room temperature trips the thermostat which is in a thin glass tube, hanging down in the water from the tank's rim. A thermostat switch in the tube turns on a heating element, also in the tube. (Some heater systems use two tubes: one for the thermostat and the other for the heater.) Aquarium heaters come in a wide range of wattages to handle tanks of any size.

An aquarium thermometer is an important part of this system. Some are floating glass tubelike units, while others snap in place inside the tank rim — with their bulb and read-out scale visible through the aquarium glass.

Most aquarium thermostat heaters and thermometers are very well made and quite accurate. But accidents do happen: A heater may fail to turn on — or worse — may fail to turn *off*! The latter situation could be drastic if the heater were too powerful for the tank, so it is wise never to buy a heater unit that is meant for a larger tank than the one you use it in.

When selecting a heater, if the room where the tank is to be located never gets below 65°F — and you want to keep the tank at 75°F — you will want a heater unit able to raise the water temperature about 10°F. It takes about 4 watts of power to raise each gallon of tank water 10°F. Therefore, if you have a twenty-gallon tank, it would take about 80 watts (4 watts x 20 gallons) to keep the aquarium water at 75°F in a room that is ten degrees cooler. Two 50-watt heaters, or a single 100-watt heater, will be enough to hold the aquarium at 75°F.

Two 50-watt heaters are a better choice than one of 100 watts. Their advantage is that it is most unlikely that both heaters might stick "on," raising the water temperature to an unsafe level. Only one heater — of 50 watts — stuck "on," couldn't overheat the tank. The second heater — still operating properly — would simply remain off and so prevent any major rise in temperature.

Another reason for using two "half-capacity" heaters, has to do with the chance that a heater might fail to turn on when there's a temperature drop. Should one unit fail to turn on, the other unit will stay on and thus not let the water temperature fall too low.

When selecting heaters, pay for the better ones, and *never* use heaters whose surplus output is enough that they could raise your tank water to temperatures above 90°F — should they fail to turn off.

CLEANLINESS depends on the filter system.

Many processes of cleanliness in the natural environment cannot be adequately duplicated in the aquarium. These conditions include sunlight, vast amounts of flowing water, space, and great numbers of green plants and microorganisms that play a role in keeping their world clean.

Considering the size of your aquarium, it usually contains more fish life than it does the other kinds of small animal forms, plants, and microorganisms that would normally contribute to cleanliness. For this reason, filters have to be used to make up for the difference.

Filters clean water as it flows through a material that screens out floating matter, and then through a layer of charcoal below that helps rid the water of certain dissolved waste materials. The clean water is then returned to the aquarium.

Many aquarium filters are plastic boxlike units that hang on the outside of the aquarium or rest inside on the gravel floor. Outside filters are equipped with several curved plastic tubes that siphon water out of the aquarium into the filter box. The water flows down through the filtering material and charcoal, where a small motor-

The thermostatically controlled heater goes in one corner, and the thermometer should be located where it can be easily seen.
Backstage in the aquarium is where all the equipment goes. A gang outlet provides a single place in which to plug all electrical items, leaving only one plug to go to a wall outlet.

driven turbine pump returns the clean water to the tank. The filtering material is usually white; when dirt darkens it, it is time to change the filtering material or wash it out.

The inside filter, being right in the water, draws water through its filter material and charcoal, using an air stream from an outside air pump to move the water through it. Of the two, the outside filter is easier to service, can handle much larger volumes of water, and is the best type of filter for large aquariums.

Another style, called the undergravel filter, is perhaps more in keeping with natural processes. Usually it is a perforated plastic sheet placed on the floor of the aquarium, under the bottom layer of gravel. Another version uses a network of perforated plastic tubing buried in the gravel. Moved by an air stream from a pump, water is drawn down through the gravel where the particulate matter (small particles) is trapped. The action of plant growth and microorganisms in the gravel promotes the breakdown of waste matter in the water — and that trapped in the gravel — and thus cleans the water that returns to the tank above the gravel. Rooted plants reuse these processed wastes (nitrates and other minerals), as do the microorganisms in the gravel.

In a tank that is not too crowded with life, this kind of filter can operate for indefinite periods. While the subgravel filter is quite effective, it is best not used in a tank with fish that like to dig up the gravel. For such active fish, only a high-output turbine filter can keep the tank reasonably clear.

Whatever filter you select it is limited in its capacity. The system as a whole can support only so much life. If you have to clean the filter material more than once a week, you've a pretty busy tank.

WATER MOVEMENT takes place naturally in the home environment of tropical fish. These are, of course, quiet bodies of water, where water movement is less pronounced than in a moving river. But few fish could accustom themselves to the dead calm of an aquarium if filters and airstones weren't employed. Of greater importance, only a very few fish could live in an aquarium where there was not enough water movement to keep the water well aerated.

(35)

Aquarium filters keep the water moving as part of the filtration process. Most hang-on units have return nozzles that can be aimed in such a way as to create a constant current of flowing water in the aquarium. This flow allows for a free exchange at the water's surface of waste gases and the reoxygenation of the tank water.

Bubbling air serves the same purpose: carrying water — pulled up by the rising bubbles — to the surface, where the waste gas and air exchange takes place.

Most aerators sold today are small diaphragm pumps designed to pump air for one or two airstones. The airstone is usually a porous stone material, on the end of a piece of rigid plastic tube. The flexible air-line tube attaches onto this tube, and the stone is dropped into the tank near the bottom. The stone creates a fine mist of bubbles in the water, which enhances the pumping action.

Where more air is needed, piston pumps are used. These are a bit more costly, but they can handle a great many more airstones or filter units that operate on air pressure.

CHANGING WATER is sometimes a crucial procedure.

Nothing is more frightening than a tank that looks like someone put a handful of flour into it along with several dead fish, and the rest looking quite ill. Those fish remaining usually are at the surface, gasping for air. Overfeeding can cause this condition, as can a dead fish that lies unnoticed in the vegetation. As the food breaks down, wastes in the water consume the available oxygen and life becomes impossible for the fish.

The first order of business is to get an airstone going in the tank to bubble air which circulates the water and increases surface gas exchange. Then turn *off* the heater and filter: You're going to do an instant water change — of about half of the water in the tank. The heater must be off while it is out of the water.

New water going into a tank should be aged several days. In this situation, you will not be able to wait. You must get the fouled water out and the new water in as quickly as possible. You *will* have to match carefully the temperature and the pH of the new water with the old. But this won't take too much time.

(36)

With the electrical items off, siphon out at least half the water in the tank and discard it. Then wash your hands since the water is polluted (make sure there is no soap left on them after rinsing). Turn on the taps strongly in a laundry sink, or the bathtub, and try to adjust the stream temperature to the same as in the tank. Put a clean bucket under the tap, and then use your thumb to create a very strong spray action of the water flowing into the bucket — enough so that it really froths as it flows and fills the pail. This action will rid the water of most of the chlorine that may be present. Carefully pour this water into the tank — and repeat the process until the tank is full. Be sure to attend to pH matters if necessary *before* adding the water to the tank.

When the aquarium is once again full, turn on the filter. Turn on the heater, and keep the added airstone going for a while. If the tank is clear again, after several hours of filtration, you should be home free.

A crisis isn't the only occasion for changing water. If you have a particularly crowded tank and need to make frequent filter changes, you should occasionally make partial changes of water: about a quarter of the tank every two or three weeks. Even though the aquarium looks clean, the filter cannot process all forms of waste. These will collect, and quickly in a crowded tank. There is less need to rush in this case. You can let the water from the tap stand in buckets to age it. But if you are in a location that does not heavily chlorinate the drinking water, the process described earlier for the instant water change will be quite safe.

LIGHT is an important factor in the aquarium. The plants used in the aquarium contribute to more than just its appearance. They add some oxygen to the water, remove some of the carbon dioxide, and help to clean the aquarium by using up converted waste product nutrients and minerals.

Most aquarium lamp housings fit snugly in place on the rim of the tank. Tungsten and fluorescent lamps are used in aquarium lamp housings — sometimes both kinds are in one housing. Using both kinds of lamps enhances the appearance of the aquarium. There

A well-stocked pet store.

are special fluorescent lamps designed to improve the growth of plantlife.

In general, the fishes' reaction to the lights is one of indifference but some fish do not like too much illumination. They are startled when the lights on the tank are turned on and off: like the sun suddenly coming up with a leap — or disappearing just as quickly. Until they get used to it, it is best not to turn on their light until daylight illuminates the room. At night, it is best to leave the room lights on, until after you've turned off the tank lights. This will make the transition to darkness a little less abrupt for your fish. Try to avoid turning on their tank lights during the night hours. This sudden deluge of light can be the most unsettling of all — even to fish long accustomed to their aquarium home. Think about it: If you woke up in the night with your room light suddenly put on, and the room full of people, wouldn't this upset *you*!

AQUARIUM ACCESSORIES are an interesting field for exploration. A visit to an aquarium store will reveal racks full of equipment, materials, chemicals, and fish foods designed to support the aquarist's hobby. But at first let the dealer advise you on just which things you really need to get started. Remember: Every gadget you buy means that much less money available to buy fish.

On the other hand many of the accessories are of obvious value — plastic tubing for air lines, air pumps of all kinds, valves, bottom-cleaning "vacuum cleaners," and scrapers to clean algae from glass walls. (Care should be taken using those that take razor blades! You can easily cut yourself and even the fish.) A piece of plastic filtering material or urethane sponge makes an excellent algae cleaner, using your hands (washed, and free of soap) to scrub down the tank.

Filter accessories include siphoning tubes equipped with screens to keep small fish from going up the tubes. Today, the most commonly used filtering material is a cottonlike polyester material (*not* cotton!). Years ago, glass wool was used, but it is unsatisfactory for, being brittle, small slivers of the glass can get into the aquarium water and be a potential hazard to the fish (not to mention your hands, while handling it.)

(39)

Activated carbon or charcoal is the other material used in the filter, and is sold in a wide variety of sizes for all kinds of filters.

A valuable accessory is a rim-mounting gang electrical outlet, with switches for turning the accessories plugged into it on and off. With the many electrical devices (pumps, heaters, etc.) needed to operate your aquarium there is an ever present shock hazard. Accessories for keeping the electrical items well-ordered are a good investment right from the beginning.

Many chemicals and health aids are available, but most chemicals and medicines have one thing in common. When *really* needed, they can be lifesavers. In the wrong amounts, they can be poisons! Follow the store dealer's advice about these materials until you've more experience in this risky area of aquarium maintenance.

The final judgment about accessories should emphasize simplicity. Keep your systems as simple as possible. Perhaps the best accessory the aquarium store has to offer is books. From these you can learn what others have gone through to make the aquarium hobby what it is today.

FOOD FOR FISHES is another essential factor. There are almost as many different kinds of foods as there are gadgets in an aquarium store. They range from all-purpose foods most fish will eat to the special diets of exotic tropical fish. The aquarium store dealer will no doubt start you off with fish that will eat conventional foods. Fortunately, most of the fish that will appeal to you initially will eat common fish food, usually a dry food that sprinkles out of its container.

Many frozen foods, such as brine shrimp, are about as easy to use and add variety to your fishes' diet, but they must be stored in the freezer compartment of your refrigerator until used.

DIFFERENT INTERESTS
AND DIFFERENT KINDS
OF AQUARIUMS

THE COMMUNITY TANK offers you the chance to observe a number of different kinds of fish at once. Your choice of fish for a community tank should be based upon which will live together in harmony. Certain fish simply cannot be put together in one tank. Some kinds may be known to eat other fish or are kinds that like to live alone. A good rule of thumb is not to mix large fish with small ones. Another has to do with mouth size: Though similar in size, fish with big mouths may attack their smaller-mouthed neighbors.

Food requirements for the fish in a community tank should be similar. Unless you've a special fondness for

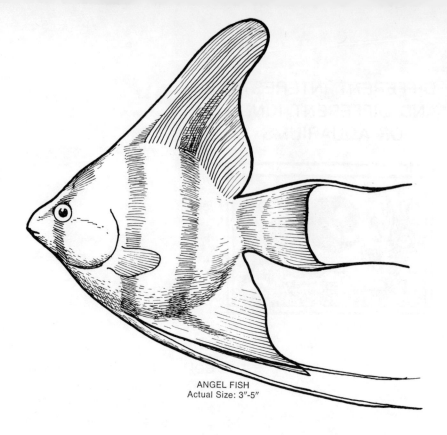

ANGEL FISH
Actual Size: 3"-5"

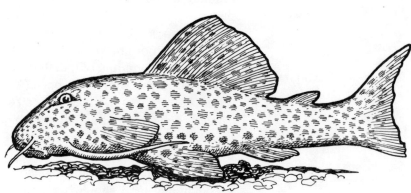

PLECOSTOMUS CATFISH
Actual Size: 2"-4"

a particular fish with a unique diet select fish for your community that share similar feeding needs. It will make your first effort a lot less involved, giving you more time to study and enjoy your aquarium. You should also select fish whose environmental requirements are less stringent during your learning period.

The community tank is very like a theater of many players, and the setting should be appropriate. The tank must not be crowded. Each fish needs its niche in there, somewhere. A twenty-gallon tank is quite acceptable. Accessories required to run the system will be about the same as those needed for a smaller tank, so the cost for the system will not be much greater.

Use your artistic imagination when setting up the tank. By careful terracing, location of rocky shelves, and using a variety of plants, you can create an artistic view into the watery world that will enhance the fish. A sword plant makes an ideal centerpiece, while Vallisneria makes a fine curtain to shield filters, heaters, and the like.

Try to create "thickets" of vegetation behind and in which fish can find refuge. While you want to see your fish, if they cannot find seclusion when they feel they need it, they may become distressed and sulk in a corner of the tank. While they may occasionally stay in the plant areas you've created, when they *do* venture forth, they will look their regal best.

Select all the fish for your community tank, but you need not buy them all at once. A few small Angel fish (*Pterophyllum eimekei,* or *scalare*) with a "house cleaning staff" — such as a Plecostomus catfish (the most vacuum-cleaner-like of all) — is a good beginning. Other housecleaners include members of the Corydoras armoured catfish. All are scavengers that spend their time picking up scraps from the tank floor. The Plecostomus is particularly fond of algae which they diligently scrub off the glass sides.

Snails also make good scavengers, and are particularly useful at cleaning up nursery tanks, for they will not disturb even very young hatchlings (but keep an eye on them in a tank of eggs!)

The snail is an important
housecleaner in an aquarium.
The Plecostomus catfish (left)
is very like a vacuum cleaner,
scrubbing down the glass
sides of the aquarium while
eating the algae that grows
there. Below right: Angel
fish (*Pterophyllum scalare*).

One or two "cats" in a community tank are sufficient. Too many rooting about the bottom can stir up an otherwise crystal clear tank.

After your first fish become established, you can begin to add the other kinds you'd like in your community. Most members of the Characin family make excellent community members. The Neon tetra (*Hyphessobrycon innesi*), the Cardinal tetra (*Cheirodon axelrodi*) and the Black tetra (*Gymnocorymbus ternetzi*) are quite attractive. These fish like to travel as a school, so a half dozen of each will create clusters of color that move about and add contrast to the overall scene.

Even with the plantings near the back of the tank, you can often see through to the clutter of the filter box, hanging wires, air tubes. You can either buy a backdrop scene from the aquarium store or use your artistic skills to paint a watery world backdrop on a piece of cardboard. It need only be random shapes of cold colors, streaks of green — all to simulate more vegetation in the distance *behind* the tank. When dry and taped in place, it will add depth to your tank and be an improvement over the hanging wires.

Maintaining your community tank should become routine: A weekly change or cleaning of filtering material, several feedings of fish food a day, a periodic check that the heaters are holding the tank somewhere near 75°F — and a watchful eye for any sign of disease among your company of aquatic actors!

THE SINGLE-SPECIES TANK is the second-most popular type of aquarium. Your enthusiasm for a particular actor may prompt you to invest in another aquarium to be devoted to this single species. The tank for a single species is little different from the community tank, as regards equipment needs, set up, plants, house cleaning life, etc. You will, however, not be dealing with a general pattern of requirements to suit many kinds of fish, so you can strive to meet more exactly the particular requirements of the one species. And if its requirements are unique, the single tank may be the only kind of tank in which the fish will do well.

A tank full of Cardinal tetras is a good example. They seem to do well in a community tank, but their home waters are very acid (near a pH of 5). So if you would enjoy this species at its best, make its aquarium as much like its natural environment as possible. A little study in preparation will make you aware of just what that environment is like; water temperature, hardness of water, pH, bottom conditions, light or dark, shallow or deep, etc. — and what it best likes to eat.

A smaller tank — say ten gallons — is usually quite acceptable for a single species (if the adult size of the fish isn't larger than a half dollar). With the tank ready you can go make your purchase. Do not be alarmed to find your chosen fish is in water not of its native pH, temperature, etc.

While floating their store bag in their new home, make your pH readings of the tank and their container. Here, any pH change needed will *not* be done as earlier directed for transferring into a community tank. If the pH difference between their new tank and their store water is more than one or two full points, you must change the pH of the small amount of water in their transfer bag to match that of their new tank. This would be difficult to do with chemicals, so ladle tank water — a few teaspoons at a time — into their transfer bag, every few minutes or so, until, over a half hour's time, their bag water is within at least a half a point of the water in their new tank. They can then be loosed into their new home.

While the fish in your single-species tank may eat conventional fish foods, try to obtain any special foods they may normally eat in their wild home — or a dietary equivalent! A great deal is being written on the subject, including single pamphlets on almost each and every tropical fish sold in aquarium stores. A little reading up on your part will start you on the right feeding program.

A single-species tank is a decided challenge. You will be using the best tools of a now well-hardwared industry to create a transplanted miniature version of the home environment of the species you've selected. The reward for your efforts may be the realization of every aquarist's dream: To breed a fish no one else has bred in an aquarium!

THE BREEDING TANK will be needed if you've really been successful with your efforts to duplicate the fishes' environmental conditions, and they prove it by breeding. Many fish, when spawning, will eat their freshly laid eggs! Or they may consume the hatchlings — known as "fry."

This strange behavior (by our standards) means only one thing: The fishes' home-away-from-home may be good, but it still isn't perfect for raising young.

What do you do if breeding takes place in a community tank — and your desire is to try to salvage the situation. The only course open to you is to turn it into a breeding tank. To do this you must try netting all other fish out of the tank — catfish and all. This often isn't successful, for trying to net out the rest of the fish may so upset the parents that they will eat the eggs as a result of the disturbance.

About the best you can do is to try, netting out those easily caught — as near to the other end of the tank as possible. Those you can't net out quietly, leave be. At least there will be fewer remaining fish for the parents to contend with. If they eat the young in spite of your efforts, make sure you know which are the parents, and then net out the other fish. In all likelihood they will breed again, later, when conditions are less crowded.

Of course moving everyone else out means setting up a new community tank; i.e., the former community tank is now going to become a breeding tank.

What changes you will make in the single-species tank (or a community tank hastily converted to a breeding tank) to make a suitable breeding tank of it will again come from reading up on the breeding behavior of the species involved. If little is known about it you will be very much on your own. Seek the advice of other aquarium-keeping friends who can help you make wise guesses.

Generally, the new requirements you are dealing with as regards breeding involve space, temperature change, places for shelter and seclusion (and more of the same for the young), and use of equipment that doesn't interfere with breeding.

The breeding behavior of tropical fish simply isn't classifiable. Their approaches to reproducing their kind are unimaginably varied — and sometimes bizarre. One species, the Egyptian mouthbreeders (*Haplochromis* multicolor), represents some sort of extreme: Once the two fish have routinely laid and fertilized the eggs, the female quickly scoops up the eggs — and all that are subsequently laid — into her oversized mouth, where they remain protected for several weeks against nature's dangers. She will eat nothing during this time! As delicate a menu as the eggs and subsequent fry might be, though she visibly wastes away, and grows thin, she does not swallow them if conditions are to her liking.

Each species has its own way of dealing with reproduction, and so you will have to contend with the needs of each kind of parent and their young as best you can.

There are always two questions to breeding fish: Do you breed the parents and raise the young in the same tank, or do you breed the parents and at some time following remove the eggs (or hatchlings) to yet another tank that will serve as a nursery — away and secure from the chance the parents will consume them?

The former is nature's way — and the best testimonial to your success at creating a complete home environment for the fish. A pair of Oscars (*Astronotus ocellatus*) surrounded by a sea of their young is a most pleasing sight. Oscars are a species that often make excellent parents, provided their space isn't allowed to become gradually crowded, as their young grow in size.

☐ *Space* is a key factor. While the breeding tank may be quite adequate for the parents, the eggs, and the very young hatchlings — often in the thousands — that same space grows smaller as the young increase in size — until the parents may solve the shrinking space problem by eating the young! So it is important to keep track of the behavior of the parents so that you know, in time, to move the young out if the parents show signs of frustration.

☐ *Temperature* can play an important role in the breeding process. A planned change in temperature can trigger breeding in tropical fish. An abrupt but slight several-degree increase in temperature can simulate what in nature would be the effect of warm rains flowing off the land into the river and stream homes of tropical fish. This is the time when many fish breed. You can create this condition in the aquarium by pouring a pitcher or so of warm water — as much as 110°F — into their tank until its overall temperature rises three or four degrees. (Pour it in at some location *away* from the fish!) There are indications that other happenings in nature, such as lightning and thunder, can play an equally stimulating role. While this can be hard to duplicate in a city apartment building, repeated flashing of a photographic strobe light (electronic flash) at the same time warm water is poured into their tank — in semidarkness — enhances the effort to stimulate breeding.* The strobe light, though quite intense, does not adversely disturb the fish as does turning on their tank light in the dead of night.

☐ *Places for shelter and seclusion* are important for the breeding fish. The breeding tank should be in a secluded area of your home or school. When fish breed, their sense of territory becomes quite pronounced. Faces peering into their tank suggest a threat to their young. In a sense, the space *in* your living room, near their tank, may become part of their "territory" and to invade it may doom their young. Should breeding happen in a community tank in your living room, or anywhere your family is frequently present and active, and should you decide to turn it into a breeding tank — you may have to put up a screen *near* their tank, to prevent activity in the room from disturbing them. But do not put the screen so close to the glass as to make them feel cramped or — worse yet — paste paper over the glass to shut out the room. This could give them a genuine case of claustrophobia!

* The author has produced a high incidence of fish-breeding activity immediately following the simulation of storm conditions, including the playing of thunderstorm sound effects recordings. The fish used in these experiments were *Astronotus o.*

Breeding Oscars:
A pair of Oscars
with a clutch of eggs.
In several days the
eggs hatch, and the
young fish are soon
swimming in a cloud
around their parents,
who jealously guard
them from harm.

Young Oscars, (here enlarged) are about a quarter of an inch long.

☐ *Shelter for the young* is equally important for some species. Provide thickets of plantings and other dense vegetation where the young can hide if the parents should make a darting pass at one of their young. In the case of Oscars, slabs of slate or rock, must be used, for Oscars will dig up any and all plants put in their tank.

☐ *Tank equipment must be baby-proofed.* Very young fish somehow find their way into the filter, unless the siphon tubes are fitted with very fine mesh covers. Many more siphon tubes added to the filter box are a partial answer, for there will be less suction, per tube, and thus less chance the youngsters will be sucked up and trapped against even a screened input tube.

THE NURSERY TANK as a separate unit is the wisest choice for any aquarist who wants to be sure to rear the eggs or hatchlings of a pair of breeding fish. This may be yet another tank set up next to the breeding tank, or a tank into which the *parents* go — making the former breeding tank now a *nursery.* The question of which it shall be depends on which is easier to move — the eggs (or young) or the parents. When Neon tetras have bred — or any of those smaller fish that scatter their eggs — they are usually easily netted and removed, leaving the eggs to mature. On the other hand, while a pair of adult Oscars *can* be netted and moved to another tank, you and your living room may be well drenched with water by the time you've done the moving, for they will dart about in an effort to avoid your net. Being large fish, they may also injure themselves plunging into the glass sides of their tank — or leap right out of the tank onto the living room floor! In the case of Oscars, it is best and a bit easier to spirit their young away — although not that much easier, for they will charge the net, or dip tube — or your hand — if you're trying to remove the rock on which they've laid eggs (if they haven't laid them directly on the tank's slate floor).

Conditions in the nursery tank should be identical to those in the breeding tank (temperature, pH, etc.) and the transfers should be done as an instant out-of-one-tank-and-into-the-other action. (In

Transferring the young fish: Getting the young out of the breeding tank seems an awesome task, but it's really quite easy. If another tank is nearby and at the same height, the second tank's water can be siphoned into the breeding-tank filter. This water adds to the volume — and raises the waterline — of the breeding tank. A second siphon hose is then set up to drain this added water back into the tank it came from. With it will go the youngsters, who are caught in the stream, and are quickly carried "over the hump" into their new quarters. Since there are lots of infants, it takes a day or so. But the process is the least disturbing to the adults, who, not being able to count, are none the wiser.

the case of a rock of eggs, they shouldn't be left in the open air more than a few seconds.)

Plants and gravel are not needed in the nursery tank. In fact, gravel can be a problem, as uneaten food can collect in it and spoil. If you are hatching eggs, it is best that there be only water in the tank: Your problem will be keeping fungus and other organisms in the gravel away from the eggs. The outflow of the filter, its tube aimed to flush over the rock, or whatever the eggs are on, will help wash them, or a rising stream of bubbles from an airstone will "wash" the eggs that are resting in its path. While there are still eggs in the tank, keep other creatures out. When they've hatched, and are free swimming, a Plecostomus catfish and some snails can be added to clean up uneaten food.

After a month or so the young fish can be put into a single-species tank — or you can strike up a deal with the aquarium store proprietor in order to make some money on the young that are surplus to your needs!

THE SALT WATER AQUARIUM is a unique world in itself, and, as an enclosed mini-environment, is representative of the oldest realm of life — the oceans. Salt water aquariums are very difficult to maintain. Aside from caring for the usual requirements of an aquarium, you must also contend with the salinity of the water — how much salt is in solution.

The greatest problem salt water presents is its reaction to metals and tank cements — reaction that can contaminate the water and kill its inhabitants.

While the aquarium industry has designed excellent equipment for the fresh water aquarist, it has only recently made a real effort to design equipment for handling salt water. When metal and some other materials come into contact with salt water they will break down and contaminate the system.

Until very recently, a great many aquarium products were made of such destructible materials. Many earlier turbine filter systems used metal parts that came in direct contact with the salt water. The cements used in earlier tanks would loose poisons into the salt water. And where they were made of wrought iron, it would corrode — and loose its toxic oxides into the water. And until the recent development of artificial sea salts for turning fresh water into "instant" ocean water, if your collection of beautiful ocean fish was suffering, it could mean a long trip to the ocean — perhaps in the dead of winter! Unless you were willing to make the trip to get new water, you could lose some very expensive fish. But for those who care, it is worth the trouble: Few creatures are as beautiful as the fish that come from the tropical coral reefs of the world.

With new tank designs and plastics and tank sealants that are unaffected by salt water, keeping salt water aquaria is now much more within the capabilities of aquarium enthusiasts.

The aquarium maintenance techniques discussed before apply equally to the salt water aquarium, with the added physical factor of water density to be considered. Sea water contains dissolved salts; not just table salt, but many kinds. A special tool, called a hydrometer, is used to measure the density of the salts. As water evaporates from the tank, the salts remain and so the tank's water density increases. When pure water is added to the tank, the hydrometer is used to determine how much to add in order to restore the desired water density. Instead of regular tap water that often contains some salts, use distilled water (most drug stores sell it) to make up for evaporative loss.

Water filters must be those that contain no metals that come into contact with the aquarium's salt water. The same goes for any of the equipment that is used *in* the tank: Heaters that use plastic rim clamps are better than those that use aluminum clips. Though they do not usually reach into the water, water spraying onto them reacts with the metal and drips back into the tank and contaminates it.

All-glass tanks are best equipped with a full glass cover with

The salt water aquarium: The marine tank is a challenge for even the most experienced aquarist. The challenge is worth it, when you've mastered dealing with the special requirements of the marine tank, for many ocean fish are truly splendid, such as the Clown fish, *Amphiprion percula,* right.

A stunning creature of the seas — but quite dangerous, the Lion fish *(Pterois volitans)* is equipped with spines which can puncture the flesh and release a painful venom when touched. Right: Though it looks like a flowering plant, the sea anemone is a sea creature whose tentacles are equipped to capture small fish that happen too close.

plastic hinged ports to allow access inside. The lamp housing goes on top of the glass. In this way salt mist that collects on the glass (usually from the spray of an airstone) drips back into the tank — uncontaminated.

Because the equipment and tank requirements are more complicated, this salt water phase of the aquarium hobby is best delayed until you've become quite familiar with keeping fresh water tropical fish, and have gained the experience needed to take on this more complicated form of the hobby.

HEALTH IN THE AQUARIUM must always be kept in mind. Bad health visits any creature from time to time. But a well-maintained tank is seldom visited by pestilence: The best defense against disease in a tank is vigorous, healthy fish. This is why attending to fishes' requirements is so important. If any are not given adequate attention — such as keeping the temperature just right — those fish affected by improper temperature may become so weak they cannot ward off disease.

There are too many disorders that afflict tropical fish to discuss them here, but there are books and pamphlets available that consider them in detail. A great many illnesses stem from neglect that allows the physical environment to change beyond the ability of the fish to tolerate the condition. But certain physical conditions can also help them to get well.

Increasing water temperature can frequently arrest a disorder, or play an important part in the cure process. Ick, described earlier, is one disorder that often comes about when an aquarium is allowed to drop to a low temperature for the particular species involved. Many parasitic organisms cannot thrive if the tank water is slowly elevated to about 85°F. It can be raised even higher with some fish. Where medicines are available to treat a specific ailment, the elevated temperature can hasten recovery. Manuals of fish care will give you specific details.

Water movement can play a healthy role in an aquarium. Many

Aquarium photography: Taking pictures of a tank of attractive tropical fish is part of the hobby. Even a box camera — with closeup attachments — can be used. Of course using better equipment makes the job easier. While light from directly overhead is quite effective — the photos of Oscars elsewhere in this book were so shot — two side lights with an all-glass tank tend to cut down the contrast. So also does a ripple-glass cover tend to diffuse single overhead lighting.

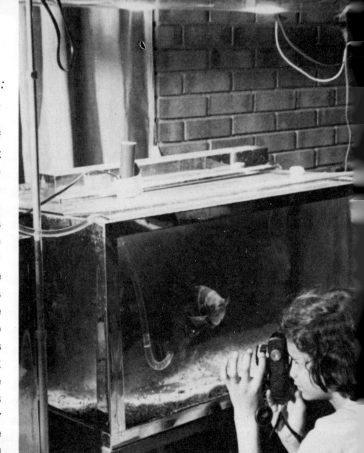

parasitic organisms live part of their lives in the soil. When they invade the body of the fish during the next phase of their life, the fish becomes ill. When a microorganism leaves the soil (or other location) stage of its life, it usually must find its new host in a short period of time. While it can swim, it is more difficult for it to do so in moving water. A turbine filter is quite useful in this respect: It keeps the water moving fast enough that the parasite cannot find its new host — a fish — before it perishes.

Adding salt to aquarium water can destroy certain microorganisms. Since many kinds of aquarium fish come from coastal streams laden with some ocean water, they can stand having salt added to their water to kill microorganisms. When reading about the various kinds of disorders that afflict fish, you will find that many remedies include adding non-iodized salt to the aquarium water.

But the best defense against health problems is to avoid them — by keeping the aquarium clean, attending to all the fishes' physical needs, and keeping them well fed.

You should take care that you do not put anything into the tank that could cause health problems — such as a newly acquired fish that doesn't appear healthy. Such a fish should be kept in another tank until you know it is healthy enough to add to your collection.

When treating illnesses the use of medicines becomes a last resort. Some of the chemicals and medicines available at the aquarium store can be very effective solutions to certain disorders. Unfortunately, some can be very hard on other life in the aquarium, so when using a given medicine make sure that other life in the tank won't be affected. For example, certain medicines will effectively treat an ailment — but will kill all the plants and snails. Aquarium stores now pay more attention to tropical fish ailments, and much is written on the matter, so between the aquarium store proprietor's experience and the reading material he has on hand, you can usually treat any diseases that afflict your community of tropical fish.

Two small strobelites were used to take the Oscar pictures. The tank was fifty gallons, so two lamps were needed to keep illumination even throughout the tank. (One light is enough for smaller tanks). The lamps were held 18 inches above the ripple-glass cover. Panatomic X film was used (developed in Microdol 3:1 dilution) with an exposure of 1/125 of a second (to make sure other lighting in the room would not be included) at an F stop of 5.6. KII Kodachrome taken at the same time was shot at F3.5 & F4.

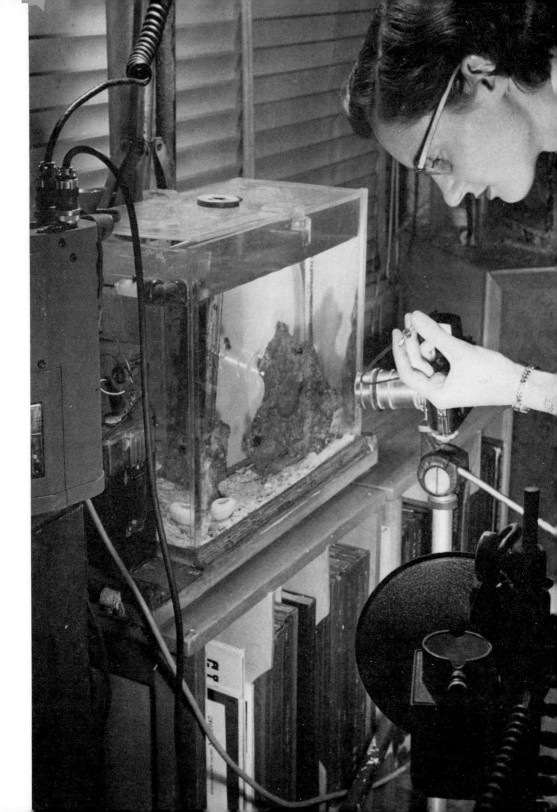

INDEX

ABOUT THE AUTHOR

John Hoke majored in biology at Antioch College. He is especially interested in wildlife and photography, and often combines the two interests in his books. He is currently working with the National Park Services on projects to improve urban environments by restoring natural elements to our cities. Mr. Hoke's other books include *Terrariums, Ecology,* and *Solar Energy.*

639
HOK
Hoke, John

Aquariums

225

DATE		
MAR 1979		
APR 13 '82		
FEB 7 '86		
FEB 21 '86		
MAY 1990